Why Do I Feel Hungry?

and other questions about the digestive system

by

Sharon Cromwell

Photographs by

Richard Smolinski, Jr.

Series Consultant

Dan Hogan

MOONDRAKE

First published in Great Britain by Moondrake
Halley Court, Jordan Hill, Oxford OX2 8EJ,
a division of Reed Educational & Professional Publishing Ltd

OXFORD FLORENCE PRAGUE MADRID ATHENS MELBOURNE
AUCKLAND KUALA LUMPUR SINGAPORE TOKYO IBADAN
NAIROBI KAMPALA JOHANNESBURG GABORONE
PORTSMOUTH NH (USA) CHICAGO MEXICO CITY SAO PAULO

First published 1997

01 00 99 98 97
10 9 8 7 6 5 4 3 2 1

ISBN 0 431 06158 0

British Library Cataloguing in Publication Data

Cromwell, Sharon
  Why do I feel hungry? – (Body wise)
  1. Human anatomy – Juvenile literature   2. Human physiology –
  Juvenile literature   3. Body, Human – Juvenile literature
  I. Title
  612

Printed and bound in Malaysia by Times Offset (M) Sdn. Bhd.

Contents

Some words are shown in bold, **like this**. You can find out what they mean by looking in the Glossary.

What happens to the food I eat?

Do you know what happens to food after you chew it and swallow it? First, it travels down your throat. Then it goes through a pipe called the **oesophagus** (ih-sah-fah-gus), and into your stomach. From there, it moves through a long, tube-like **organ** called the small intestine. As it moves, the food is broken down more and more.

The food's **nutrients** are taken in through your intestine walls. Those nutrients give your body energy and help it grow. This is called **digestion**.

BODY FACT
The best way to get all the nutrients your body needs is to eat plenty of vegetables and fruits.

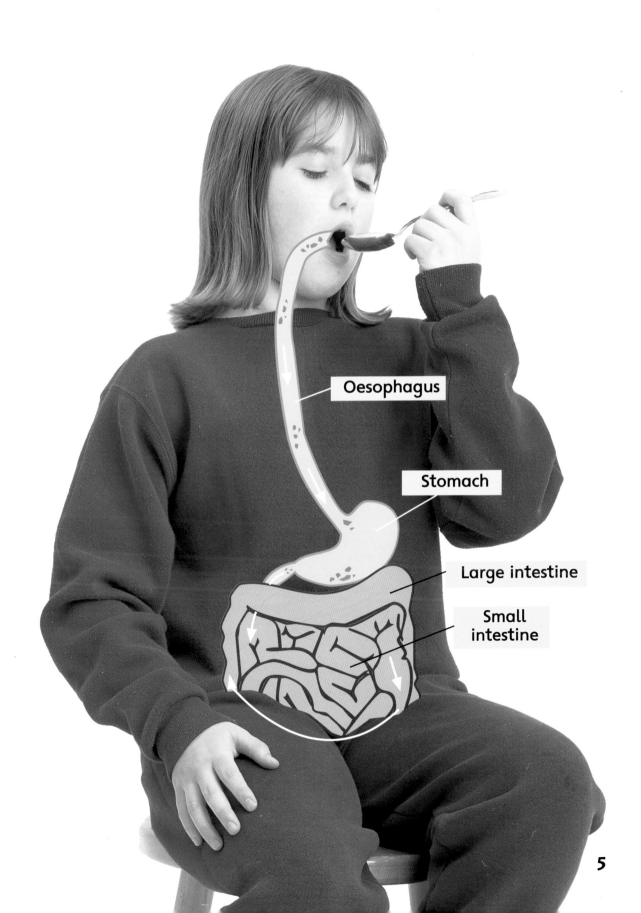

Oesophagus

Stomach

Large intestine

Small intestine

How do I digest food?

Digestion really begins when you start chewing. As you chew, the liquid in your mouth, called **saliva**, starts to break down food. In your stomach, other liquids break down the food even more. From your stomach, food passes into your small intestine.

Inside the small intestine, food is broken down into smaller bits. These bits are so tiny they can pass from the small intestine right into your blood vessels.

Some food cannot be digested. It passes into the large intestine. Your body then gets rid of this leftover food, or waste, through the **anus**.

BODY FACT

After you eat a meal, try to choose a quiet activity to do. This will help you to digest your food.

Why do I feel hungry?

Air moving around in your stomach causes rumbling that you can hear. ("Tummy" and "stomach" mean the same thing.)

BODY FACT

Food usually stays in your stomach for three to four hours. That's why you need to eat a meal or snack about every four hours during the day.

1 Your stomach and your intestines move all the time.

2 When all the food is gone from your stomach or intestines, air fills those parts of your body.

3 As muscles in your stomach and intestines move the air around, the moving air makes a rumbling sound.

4 Then your tummy rumbles, and you know you're hungry!

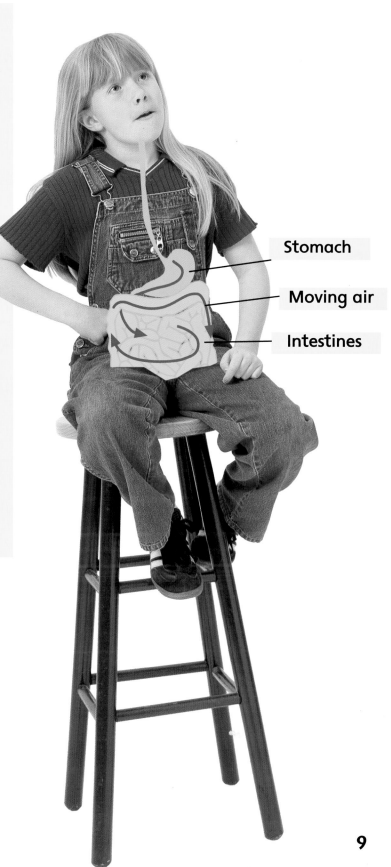

Stomach

Moving air

Intestines

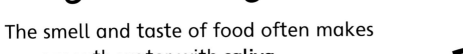

Why does my mouth water?

The smell and taste of food often makes your mouth water with **saliva**.

BODY FACT

Your teeth are covered with enamel. This is the hardest material in your body. But, if you don't clean your teeth well, **bacteria** from old food can damage this enamel.

1 The smell of food reaches your brain.

2 Your brain sends a message to your salivary **glands** telling them to produce saliva.

3 Once you begin to eat, chewing causes more saliva to be produced.

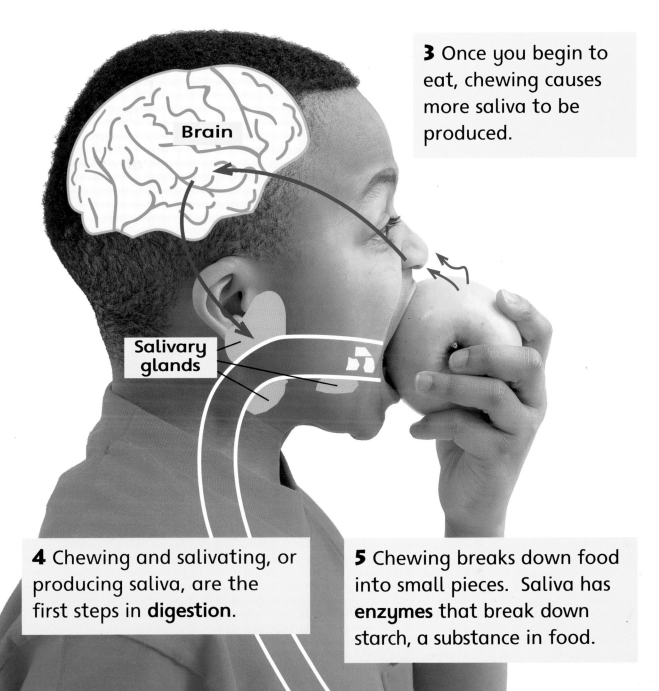

Brain

Salivary glands

4 Chewing and salivating, or producing saliva, are the first steps in **digestion**.

5 Chewing breaks down food into small pieces. Saliva has **enzymes** that break down starch, a substance in food.

What is a burp?

Air travelling up through your **oesophagus** comes out of your mouth in a burp.

BODY FACT

Burps help you digest food and feel more comfortable.

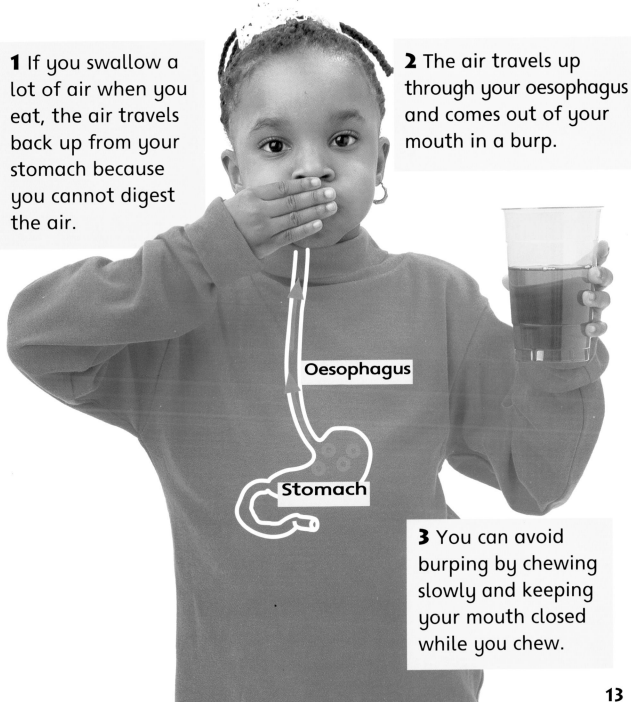

1 If you swallow a lot of air when you eat, the air travels back up from your stomach because you cannot digest the air.

2 The air travels up through your oesophagus and comes out of your mouth in a burp.

Oesophagus

Stomach

3 You can avoid burping by chewing slowly and keeping your mouth closed while you chew.

Why do I get a tummy ache when I eat too much?

The squeezing of muscles in your stomach gives you a tummy ache.

BODY FACT

Fatty foods like chips and ice cream are hard for your body to digest. If you eat meals that don't have too many fatty foods, you will feel better.

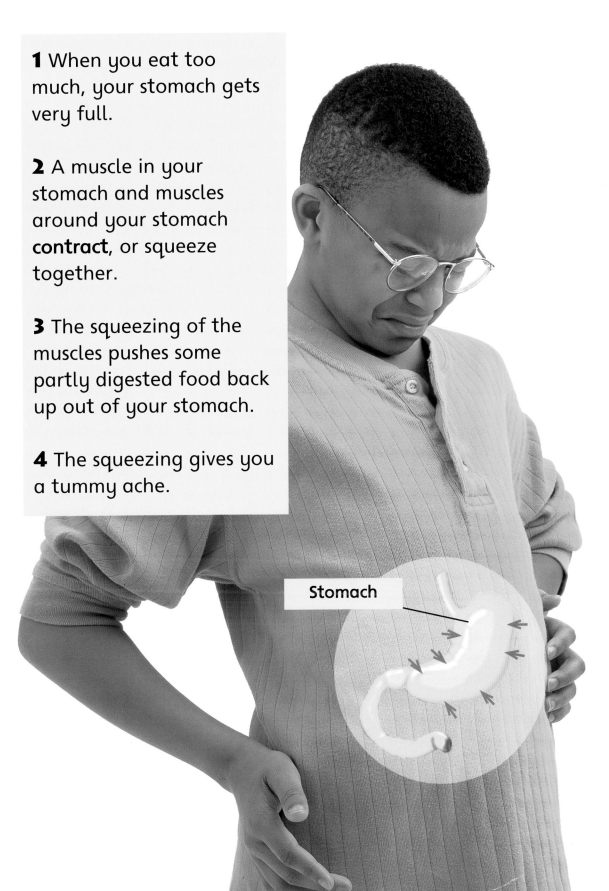

1 When you eat too much, your stomach gets very full.

2 A muscle in your stomach and muscles around your stomach **contract**, or squeeze together.

3 The squeezing of the muscles pushes some partly digested food back up out of your stomach.

4 The squeezing gives you a tummy ache.

Stomach

Why do I vomit?

A large muscle near your stomach works with the muscles in your **abdomen** to squeeze partly digested food up out of your stomach. The food travels up your **oesophagus**, and out your mouth.

BODY FACT

Vomiting can help your body get rid of something harmful, such as food that is off.

1 Maybe you've eaten or drunk too much too fast. A lot of partly digested food or liquid in your stomach can make you vomit.

2 When you have too much partly digested food in your stomach, it sends a message to a special part of your brain.

3 Your brain sends a message to your stomach that there is too much partly digested food in your stomach.

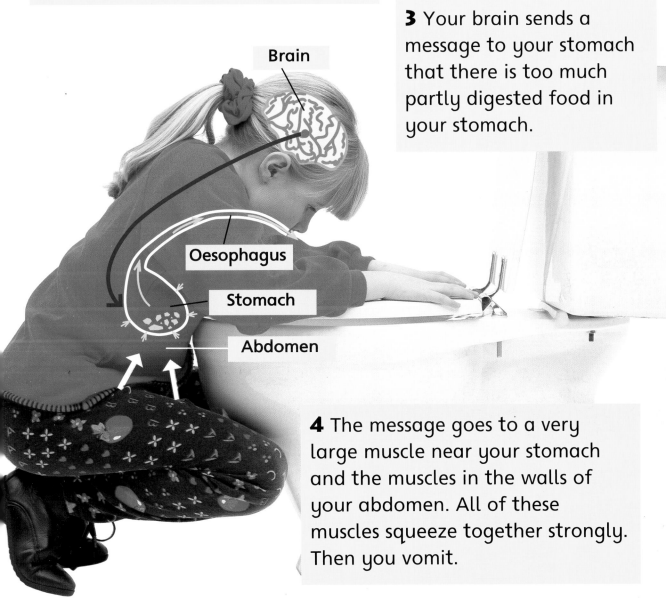

Brain

Oesophagus

Stomach

Abdomen

4 The message goes to a very large muscle near your stomach and the muscles in the walls of your abdomen. All of these muscles squeeze together strongly. Then you vomit.

Why do I pass wind?

Bacteria in your large intestine help break down food. The bacteria and partly broken down food can sometimes produce **gas.**

BODY FACT

Many foods that may produce a lot of gas are very healthy. Examples are apples, broccoli and onions.

- You have millions of bacteria in your body. Bacteria are tiny living things that you can't see. Some bacteria are harmful. Others are helpful.

- Helpful bacteria in your large intestine help break down food.

- As the bacteria break down food, gas is sometimes produced.

- When some foods, like beans, are broken down in the large intestine, a large amount of gas is produced.

- When a lot of gas builds up, it comes out through the **anus**, the opening at the end of the large intestine.

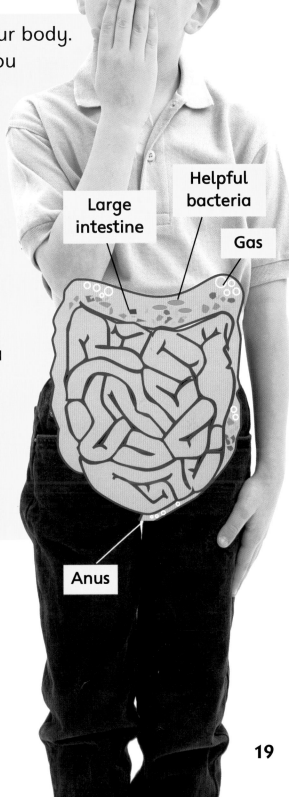

Large intestine

Helpful bacteria

Gas

Anus

Why do I go to the toilet?

You go to the toilet so that your body can get rid of liquid and solid waste.

BODY FACT

After you eat, it takes an average of 24 hours for **nutrients** to be absorbed by the small intestine.

1 Liquids and solids that cannot be digested go from your small intestine to your large intestine.

Large intestine

Small intestine

Kidneys

Bladder

Anus

2 The liquid passes into your blood vessels through the walls of the large intestine. Then the liquid is taken out of your blood by a pair of **organs** called your kidneys.

3 Next, the water goes to a bag-like organ called a bladder. Then it passes out of your body as **urine**.

4 Undigested solid food is called **faeces**. It comes out of your large intestine through your **anus**.

Explore more!
Your digestive system

1 MOUTH-WATERING MADNESS!

WHAT YOU'LL NEED:

• A handkerchief or something to use as a blindfold
• Two of your favourite foods
• One food you don't like
• A friend to help you

THEN TRY THIS!

Have your friend blindfold you. Then, one at a time, your friend should hold up a food for you to smell. Take a deep sniff. See if you salivate after smelling each food. Can you tell which foods made your mouth water the most? Did some foods not make your mouth water at all?

3 BUBBLY BURPS AND BELCHES!
WHAT YOU'LL NEED:
• Juice or water
• A fizzy drink

THEN TRY THIS!
Take a few gulps of juice or water. Do you feel a burp inside? Then take a few gulps of something fizzy. Feel the air inside create a burp. You can let it out in a great big BURP!

2 ARE YOU A TRUE-BLUE CHEWER?
WHAT YOU'LL NEED:
• Some bread to chew.

THEN TRY THIS!
Take a big bite of bread and chew it without swallowing. Keep chewing and chewing. Soon the bread will start to taste sweet. This is because an **enzyme** in your **saliva** turns the starch in bread into sugar.

Glossary

abdomen – the part of your body between the bottom of your chest and your hips

anus – the opening at the end of the large intestine

bacteria – tiny living things that are all around you and also inside your body

contract – to make smaller by squeezing together

digestion – the breaking down of food into tiny parts

enzymes – substances in your body that help break down food

faeces – undigested solid food that passes out of your body through your **anus**

glands – organs that make materials for the body to use

nutrients – the things in food that keep you healthy and help you grow

oesophagus – the tube that carries food from the throat to the stomach

organ – a part of the body that does one job

saliva – liquid released by the **glands** in your mouth that begins the breakdown of food

urine – liquid waste taken out of your body by the kidneys

Index